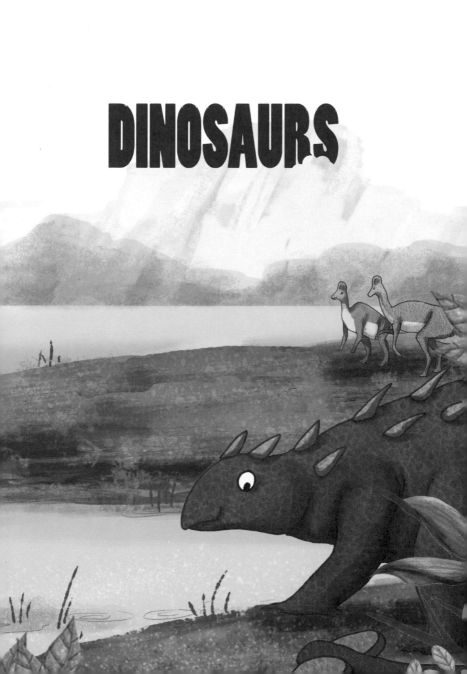

DINOSAURS

DINOSAURS

Written by **DAVID LONG**
Illustrated by **NICOLA O'BYRNE**

Orion
Children's Books

First published in Great Britain in 2015
by Orion Children's Books
an imprint of Hachette Children's Group
and published by Hodder and Stoughton Limited
Orion House
5 Upper Saint Martin's Lane
London WC2H 9EA
An Hachette UK Company

1 3 5 7 9 10 8 6 4 2

ISBN 978 1 4440 1544 7

A catalogue record for this book is available
from the British Library.

Printed and bound in China

www.orionbooks.co.uk

*To Olivia Walsh
David Long*

*For Laura x
Nicola O'Byrne*

CONTENTS

1
What is a dinosaur?

Can you imagine anything more scary
than meeting a hungry dinosaur
looking for its lunch?

Luckily this could never happen because dinosaurs disappeared more than 60 million years before the first humans were born.

But even though they lived so long ago,
we can find out lots about them.

Elephants seem enormous to us but the biggest dinosaurs weighed more than 13 or 14 elephants put together.

Think of a bus driving down the street where you live. Some dinosaurs were more than twice as long as that.

Others were taller
than a house.

Many had teeth which were so long that
if you found one and put it in your
pocket more than half of it
would stick out of the top.

These extraordinary creatures ruled
the earth for more than

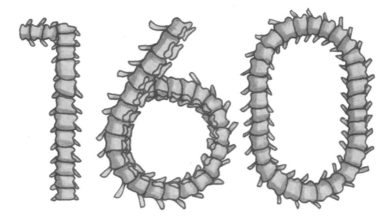

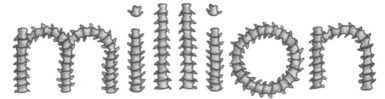

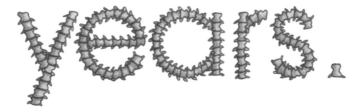

That is far longer than humans
have been alive.

Now there are no dinosaurs left people sometimes think they must have been a bit like giant crocodiles, or dragons in stories. But actually they were even more amazing than that.

2
How do we know about dinosaurs?

No-one has ever seen a living dinosaur
so you might wonder how we know
so much about them.

The answer is by studying fossils such as

the bones,

eggs

and poo

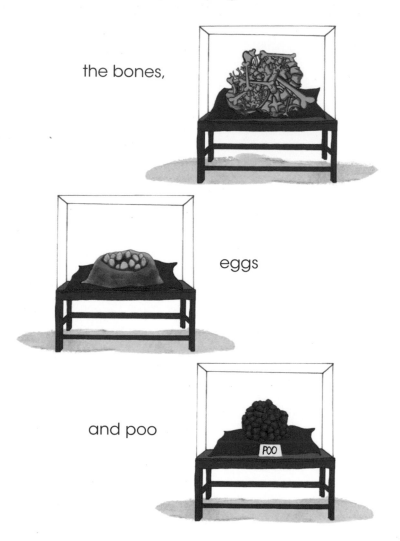

that dinosaur hunters have discovered
and you can see in museums.

After millions of years it is very unusual
for anyone to find a whole skeleton.

Often only tiny pieces or a single bone
are discovered but we can still learn
a lot from these.

From a dinosaur's poo
we can work out what it ate.

GURGLE!

The size of its skull helps us measure how big its brain was. Sometimes this could be very small (maybe no larger than a lemon).

skull

lemon

Can you guess the length of the biggest dinosaur bone ever found? It was discovered in Argentina and is larger than a fully grown man.

Much smaller ones have been found in Britain too, and a few years ago in China more than 7000 dinosaur bones were found in one place.

These different fossils show us
that there were many kinds of dinosaur.
How many can you think of?

For most people the answer is only about 4 or 5. But if you had been walking around 100 million year ago, you would have seen more than 750 different species.

As long as you managed not to get eaten by something first!

3
Did dinosaurs all eat each other?

The word dinosaur means **terrible lizard**
but this was not completely true.
Like crocodiles, they were actually reptiles
and not all of them were terrible.

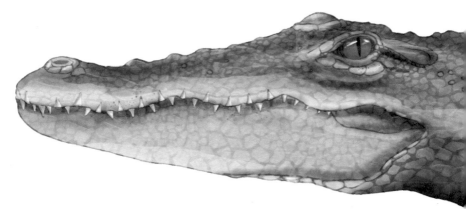

Many dinosaurs were **herbivores**.
This means they only ate plants and flowers
and had teeth that were good for eating
leaves rather than killing animals
or tearing meat.

The plant-eating **Brachiosaurus** (brak-ee-o-sore-us) was one of the largest animals ever to walk on land.

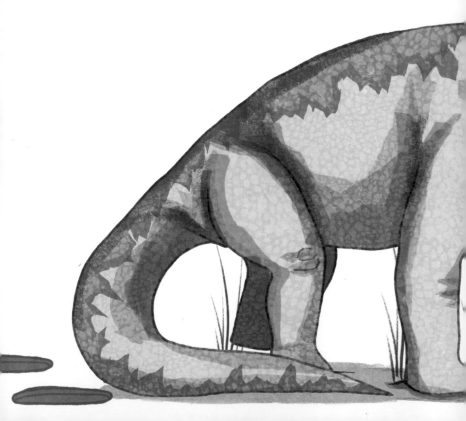

It weighed as much as 70 or
80 cars. More than 12 metres tall,
it could munch away quietly
at the tops of trees like
an enormous giraffe.

But not every herbivore was peaceful.
Triceratops (try-seh-rah-tops) had
bony shields protecting its head
and neck and also sharp horns
to drive off other dinosaurs which
tried to attack it.

Another herbivore called **Ankylosaurus** (an-kie-low-sore-us) had a heavy club on the end of its tail which it used as a weapon.

Other dinosaurs had long whippy tails to defend themselves.

The dinosaurs which ate meat are called **carnivores**. These were the most fierce ones, with heavy armour, huge claws and strong jaws. The carnivores would fight other dinosaurs and hunt down their prey.

Tyrannosaurus Rex (tie-ran-o-sore-us recks)
is the most famous of the carnivores.
It was a powerful killer with an immense
head and jaws strong enough to bite
through bone.

Their skeletons can be more than
14 metres long.

Not all of the carnivores were this big.
The **Eoraptor** (ee-o-rap-tor) is the oldest
dinosaur we know about, but it was
only 30 centimetres tall.

Although it was small it was much
faster than an Olympic runner.
It had curved teeth and long, sharp
claws to catch and hold its prey.

When they needed to be fast,
most carnivores ran on their hind legs,
using their thick, scaly tails to balance.

But others like the **Ornithosuchus** (or-nee-tho-soo-kuss) spent a lot of the time walking around on all fours.

With so many different kinds of dinosaur it is no wonder they ruled the world for so long.

4
How did dinosaurs live?

Some names of dinosaurs tell us
about how they lived.

Oviraptor (o-vee-rap-tor) means **egg thief**.
Can you guess why it was called this?

The first oviraptor skull ever found was smashed to pieces, possibly by an angry dinosaur protecting its nest.

Herbivores often lived in herds for protection,
like sheep or cows do now.

Carnivores also lived in herds but this was because hunting in packs made them more dangerous.

Working as a team a group of **Coelopysis** (see-low-fy-sis) could kill animals much larger than they were.

As fast runners they were good at chasing but like wolves today they needed others to help them pull bigger animals to the ground.

Some carnivores were big enough to hunt alone, with long claws and jagged teeth for tearing meat.

Others were scavengers which ate
the remains of any bodies they found.

55

Some dinosaurs used their strong sense of smell or hearing to hunt.

Others such as the **Troodon** (true-don) had very large eyes to spot prey in the distance.

We know this from the shape of its skull. What we don't know is whether it saw the world in colour or just black and white.

Dinosaur mothers all laid eggs but most were too big and heavy to sit on them.

Lots of species cared for their young when they were hatched.

The name **Maiasaurus** (mi-ya-sore-us)
means **good mother**. She had up to
25 babies at a time and they stayed
with her until they were more than
a metre and a half tall.

It's exciting to think that there are still many other kinds of dinosaurs waiting to be discovered.

5
Why did the dinosaurs all disappear?

We know a lot about how dinosaurs lived, but it is still a mystery why they died out. Scientists have tried to explain it in different ways.

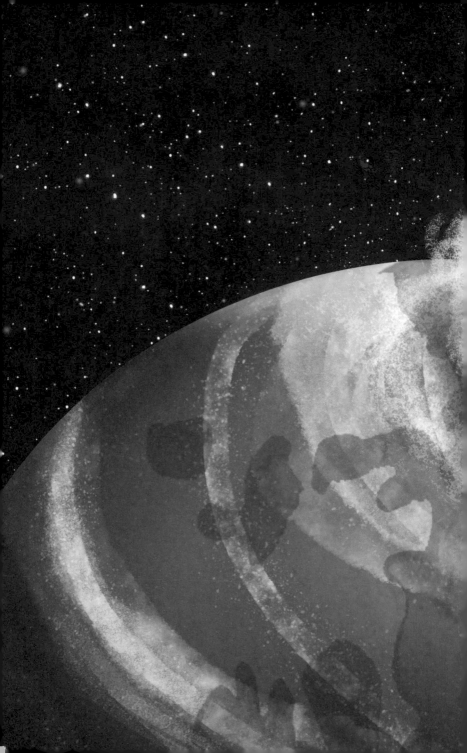

It might have been because
another planet, smaller than ours,
crashed into the earth causing a
gigantic dust cloud. This would have
blocked out the sun for years
and many plants and animals
would have died from the
bitterly cold weather.

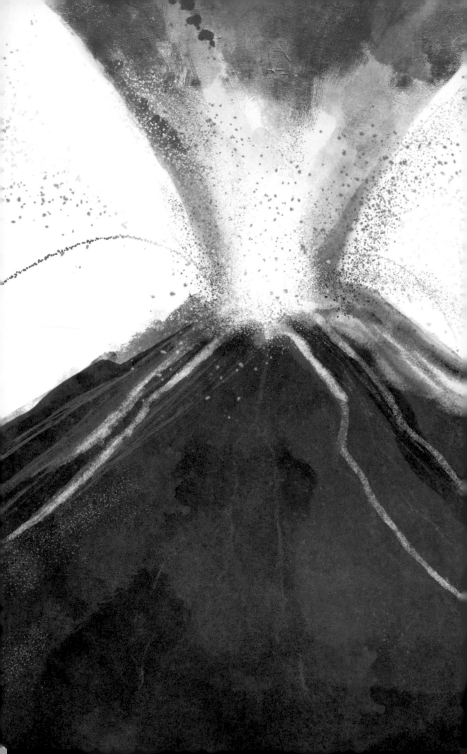

Another idea is that the climate became too hot for the dinosaurs. Millions of years ago there were many more volcanoes than there are now. The hot gases and boiling lava might have made the world so hot that the dinosaurs couldn't survive.

Whatever the reason the greatest ever reptiles all died out. Today, surprisingly, their nearest living relatives are not crocodiles or alligators or even snakes but ordinary birds.

6
When did this happen?

250
MILLION YEARS
AGO

The **Triassic** (Tri-assik) period begins.

The world is a hot, dry place.

The first dinosaurs are small and fast.
They run on their hind legs and eat meat
from other animals they manage to catch.

225 MILLION YEARS AGO

Huge, dark forests grow in the wetter climate of the **Jurassic** (Jur-assik) period. The forests are home to even larger plant-eaters, long-necked dinosaurs which walk slowly on four legs. These are hunted by ferocious carnivores, which are stronger and faster than ever.

200 MILLION YEARS
AGO

The cooler **Cretaceous**
(Cret-ay-shuss) period sees dinosaurs of
all shapes and sizes. Ferocious hunters
known as raptors with huge teeth,
strong jaws and deadly curved claws
prey on other dinosaurs.

200 MILLION YEARS AGO

The extinction of the dinosaurs.

65 MILLION YEARS AGO

Ten Great Dinosaurs

1. Corythosaurus (Cor-ee-tho-sorus) walked on all fours while feeding on low plants.

2. Stegosaurus (Steg-o-sorus) had huge plates on its back, probably for protection or for cooling down in hot weather.

3. Parasaurolophus (Para-soro-low-fuss) had hundreds of tiny sharp teeth for chewing tough plants.

4. Barosaurus (Bah-ro-sorus) didn't chew food but swallowed it whole before stones in its tummy ground it up.

5. Spinosaurus (Spy-no-sorus) had tall sails of boney skin.

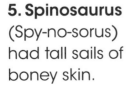

6. Daspletosaurus
(Das-plet-o-sorus)
would roar loudly
to warn other
carnivores to stay
away.

7. Sauropelta (Sore-o-pelta)
was protected by
thick skin and
had rows
of deadly
spikes.

8. Plateosaurus (Plat-ee-o-sorus)
could stand on its hind legs to reach
the leaves of tall trees.

9. Herrerasaurus (Hair-rare-a-sorus) was one of the first carnivores, from more than 200 million years ago.

10. Allosaurus (Al-o-sorus) had huge jaw muscles for crunching through bone.

WHAT WILL YOU

Dive into the deep dark sea.

Come face to face with incredible dinosaurs.

DISCOVER NEXT?

Take a look at your own back garden.

Speed off to outer space.

It's never too early to find out more.